NEW CALIFORNIA POETRY

EDITED BY

Robert Hass
Calvin Bedient
Brenda Hillman

The publisher gratefully acknowledges the generous contribution to this book provided by the General Endowment Fund of the University of California Press Associates.

FACTS FOR VISITORS

SRIKANTH REDDY

FACTS

FOR

VISITORS

POEMS

UNIVERSITY OF CALIFORNIA PRESS   BERKELEY LOS ANGELES LONDON

University of California Press
Berkeley and Los Angeles, California

University of California Press, Ltd.
London, England

For previous publication of some of the poems that appear here,
please see page 61.

Library of Congress Cataloging-in-Publication Data

Reddy, Srikanth, 1973 –
    Facts for visitors : poems / Srikanth Reddy.
        p.   cm.   —   (New California poetry ; 12)
    ISBN 978-0-520-24042-1 (cloth : alk. paper)
    ISBN 978-0-520-24044-5 (pbk. : alk. paper)
    I. Title. II. Series.
PS3618.E427 F33 2004
811'.6 — dc22   2003016067

Manufactured in Canada

13   12   11   10   09   08   07
10   9   8   7   6   5   4   3

The paper used in this publication meets the minimum requirements
of ANSI/NISO Z39.48 – 1992 (R 1997) (*Permanence of Paper*). ♾

Suzanne

CONTENTS

To Carthage then I came . . .

SAINT AUGUSTINE

BURIAL PRACTICE

Then the pulse.
Then a pause.
Then twilight in a box.
Dusk underfoot.
Then generations.

▬

Then the same war by a different name.
Wine splashing in a bucket.
The erection, the era.
Then exit Reason.
Then sadness without reason.
Then the removal of the ceiling by hand.

▬

Then pages & pages of numbers.
Then the page with the faint green stain.
Then the page on which Prince Theodore, gravely wounded,
     is thrown onto a wagon.
Then the page on which Masha weds somebody else.
Then the page that turns to the story of somebody else.
Then the page scribbled in dactyls.
Then the page which begins *Exit Angel.*
Then the page wrapped around a dead fish.
Then the page where the serfs reach the ocean.
Then a nap.
Then the peg.
Then the page with the curious helmet.

Then the page on which millet is ground.
Then the death of Ursula.
Then the stone page they raised over her head.
Then the page made of grass which goes on.

—

Exit Beauty.

—

Then the page someone folded to mark her place.
Then the page on which nothing happens.
The page after this page.

Then the transcript.
Knocking within.

Interpretation, then harvest.

—

Exit Want.
Then a love story.

Then a trip to the ruins.
Then & only then the violet agenda.

Then hope without reason.
Then the construction of an underground passage between us.

CORRUPTION

I am about to recite a psalm that I know. Before I begin, my expectation extends over the entire psalm. Once I have begun, the words I have said remove themselves from expectation & are now held in memory while those yet to be said remain waiting in expectation. The present is a word for only those words which I am now saying. As I speak, the present moves across the length of the psalm, which I mark for you with my finger in the psalm book. The psalm is written in India ink, the oldest ink known to mankind. Every ink is made up of a color & a vehicle. With India ink, the color is carbon & the vehicle, water. Life on our planet is also composed of carbon & water. In the history of ink, which is rapidly coming to an end, the ancient world turns from the use of India ink to adopt sepia. Sepia is made from the octopus, the squid & the cuttlefish. One curious property of the cuttlefish is that, once dead, its body begins to glow. This mild phosphorescence reaches its greatest intensity a few days after death, then ebbs away as the body decays. You can read by this light.

LOOSE STRIFE WITH APIARY

Watched a man watch a man. One man made smoke out of nothing by scraping together two stones. Another kept time using nothing but stones. One man made love, another made pain with a stone in each hand. Somebody take out these stitches, I'm ready to open my eyes. So this is the new world—just like the old, only brighter. Word is the governor's wife scattered loose strife in the barnyard thinking it chicken feed & the wetlands turned purple overnight. We make ready vectors for smallpox & language. Books on magnetic tape, books on bookkeeping, on being, on coping & beekeeping—I could have told you, all it takes is a meadow & nerve. Come, let me show you the recycled cosmos inside my apiary. A veil on a peg. Queen deep in the sweetness.

HOTEL LULLABY

No matter how often you knock
on the ocean the ocean

just waves. No matter
how often you enter the ocean

the ocean still says
no one's home. You must leave

her dear Ursula. As I write this
they polish the big

chandelier. Every prism
a sunset in abstract

or bijou foyer depending
on where you stand.

They take it apart every Fall
& call it Spring cleaning.

They bring me my tea.
They ask me my name

& I tell them Ursula,
I don't even know

how to miss who you left.

FIRST CIRCLE

It's dark in here, the dark inside of a man
in the dark. It's not night. One hears crows
overhead, dawn fowl caws, the shod soles again

treading their sunlit plots above. One grows
dotish-fond of such things. Long live the things,
their ways, their roots pushed goatish & gray

through the skull, in this earth that gaily spins
though one has crossed its smutted green threshold
to reign in a crate. We have done no wrong,

my friends, & yet we find ourselves soiled,
sold, carbonized teeth in a moss-riven jaw.
Once I sat on a stool as my grandmother told

me of heaven. She cleaned fish for our living. I saw
how her rusty black knife unseamed the sunset
in each belly—coral, ochre, carmine, raw,

lice-infested sunsets in a pail. So many nights.
Night in the kitchen shack, night at the crumbling edge
of our milk-pond province, a blade, lone cricket

raving in the lawn.

EVENING WITH STARS

It was light. Whoever it was
who left it under the gumtree last night
forgot to close the gate. This morning when I stepped
out on the breezeway I had to shoo off a she-pig
& three rag-pickers before I could tell
what it was they were carting away
through the leaves. I had the houseboy bear it
into the sunroom. After attending to my & my employer's
business, I returned sometime after midnight
to examine it. A pair of monkeys
were hoisting it over the threshold
toward a courtyard of fireflies. When I shook my fist
they dropped it & I settled down at last.
It was gilt. It was evening with stars.
Where a latch should have been, a latch
was painted on. Over the lid, a procession.
Chariot. Splintered tree. Chariot. Chariot.
In the lamplight the hollows
of the footsoldiers' eyes were guttering.
I'd say they looked happy.
Tired & happy. Their soil-flecked boots
sank down to the buckle in weeds
& lacquered nettles, six men to a burden.
It was light. I could see
in the middle distance a bone priest
picking his way through crop rows
toward the wreckage of an iron temple.
Scarlet clouds moving out. Jasper clouds moving in.

Here, on a cistern, a woman
keeps nursing her infant.
She is unwell.
The workmanship is astonishing.
You can pick out every lesion on her breast.

Mostly, I am alone.

SECOND CIRCLE

Now, darling. It's time you strapped me back on that wheel.
Strap me on, my salt girl, O sweet Lady Slip —
I'm down on my knees. At last I've learned how to kneel.

It's turning without me. One misses the halo, the steel
gear-teeth at the spine, the way the world flips
now, darling — it's Time. Strap me back on that wheel.

Two scarecrows faced each other across a dark field.
How do they do it? I asked the front seats, inflatable globe
on my knees. At last I've learned how. To kneel

without touching the earth, mouthing O as one reels
past the urinal doors to the dancers with whips . . .
Grave darlings of the times, you strapped me to that wheel

& I ripped myself free. Mother, you wept for a while
under the golden-red plectra of Fall & then stopped.
I'm on my knees. At last they're knees. I need them to kneel

but can't rise without you. O tie these hands, they feel
so cold they must be my hands, old things that grip
in the Now, darling. Strap me back on that wheel.
I'm on my knees at last. I've learned how to kneel.

SUNDIAL

In the hanging gardens of sleep,
they dismantled my sleep

singing from cages at daybreak.
So I entered the gardens of care,

where a boy carved in stone
kept watch on a broken stone

sundial. Care told me his story.
Had it ended sooner,

it all could have ended.
I'd have forgiven you

turning to stone without me.
When I blink, I see the blank

I carry inside me no matter
how long I keep watch.

RAVEN & ECLIPSE

The raven we'd trained to say Love stretched one bony black foot
to the scale. You said it looked like a tipsy mortician boarding a
lifeboat. I laughed but I wanted to see what it weighed. Later we
prodded until it stopped moving. As usual the X-rays were incon-
clusive though beautiful & made a fine sunshade for viewing the
next day's eclipse. I asked what exactly would be blotting out what,
but you said it depends. Can't see a thing, can't feel a thing. Think
Spring & things singing things. Did somebody say Nevermore? If
even the sky's darkest plumage keeps flashing fresh streaks of lilac
& hummingbird-green, how can I finish her likeness with only this
ocean my inkpot?

CENTAUR

who knew there would be so much
blood in a horse not the horse
not the horseman ashing
on the mudflap as he counts
three or four reds in the sunset
thinking maybe gradations
could empty one's head of a horse
when a jumbo arcs over unlacing
the clouds into mane he tosses
his boots on the flatbed & ashes
who can tell patterns from pieces
who can tell pieces from pieces
of pieces if smears on the windshield
were berries he wouldn't see wings
sprouting out of the mess
they wouldn't flutter so much
when he exits the interstate
hard by the drainage ditch swarming
with dragonflies fucking aloft

SIXTH CIRCLE

This is my latest recording. It is the sound of a man & a woman not speaking. The beauty of this silence lies in what you can hear when you turn up the volume. I have tried many times to capture this version of nothing, but women are few when one lives in this manner. Continual tears are the object. The reading of books is forbidden. Assuming an upright position is strictly forbidden. One's meals are hauled up in a bucket which can be used afterwards as a latrine & sent down again. In this manner, one's needs are satisfied. By pointing or performing simple gestures it is possible to communicate everything necessary to carry on living. A finger upraised is the firmament. The hand extended palm forward means blessing or stop.

EVERYTHING

She was watching the solar eclipse
through a piece of broken bottle

when he left home.
He found a blue kite in the forest

on the day she lay down
with a sailor. When his name changed,

she stitched a cloud to a quilt
made of rags. They did not meet,

so they could never be parted.
So she finished her prayer,

& he folded his map of the sea.

EIGHTH CIRCLE

Shadow of a bubble. Word, my world. One:
it issues from a shadow's mouth, shadow
one carries where one goes. One goes alone

& two go alone. Two: without the sun,
there would be no picnic. No picnic, no
shadow of a bubble. No word, no world. One:

it issues from a shadow's mouth, shadow
of a boy blowing soap suds in the photo
one carries where one goes. One goes alone

to visit oneself. Three: once it is blown
it casts across the blanket a mottled, hollow
shadow of a bubble. Words whirl. One:

it issues from a shadow's mouth. Shadow:
what issues from the broken box of bone
one carries where one goes? One goes alone

to the picnic. Father sits with his head of stone,
Mother weeps on the blanket. Me? I blow
the shadow of a bubble. My word, the world
one carries. Where one goes, one goes alone.

THIEVES' MARKET

They trade under a crumbling aqueduct, under meteor showers
& the red moon wired to a bitter honeysuckle stem.
Clematis has shot her root into the masonry.

They wipe ricepaper flakes & charred moths from benches
with a dripping rag; the young unpin strings of onions
hung over their stalls. Good trade, I'd say. From my lean-to

each night I hear their songpipes drifting across the canal.
Some nights I come closer, steaming in my bear suit.
I made off with a spyglass once & once with these kites.

You can have one if you sit with me until the lights go on.
Tonight they'll have fish. Fish from the rust-colored sea
hidden deep inside the jungle. Some nights they trade squid

you can slip in your pocket. Help me with this buckle, friend —
tonight I'm going in. They're lighting torches with zippos
& here come the lorries, the bullock carts. Listen.

Do you hear the whips? Broken wheels?
There's the untouchable girl I'd like to get my paws on,
the one turning handsprings at the head of the line.

She wears an amulet I've heard can stop these nosebleeds
once & for all. How her braids spin through my night!
The night is gray, my friend. Night, without middle or end.

Night. A blood-smeared beast shoulders the night.
Just give me a hand with this neck-piece, friend.
That's right. Now off you go. I can strap on the muzzle myself.

INNER LIFE

The bear stopped dancing & unscrewed his head.
He held it upside-down in the dusk. She reached
into her pouch for a copper piece, but instead
pulled out the silvery piece she'd been saving

for some special occasion. A limited issue,
stamped on one side with a profile of the prince;
on the other side a water wheel did not spin.
It glowed in her hand. Her hand grew heavy with it,

& the salts, & the bittersome oils of her hand.
Was this the occasion? The others were there
with their fists in their pouches & the weary bear
held out his head as if it were an offering

or an object lesson. It was neither. It was ripped,
with russet handfuls of animals' hair pasted on
& a secret eye slit recessed in its open maw.
The wild old man in the bear suit parted his lips

& out came a snatch of extinct birdsong.
The musicians clapped. He'd learned it as a boy
growing up in the mist-proud interior
where he would call & call until the violet males

in a frenzy swooped into his breathtaking nets.

JUNGLE BOOK

Once as we scavenged in the jungle I asked my friend
about sadness. "How will I know when it comes?"
He was up on his haunches, pulling at a leafy branch

I couldn't reach. "First learn about jackfruit," he said,
handing me a ripe one. It smelled heavy & delicate,
like my friend. "Break it. What do you see?"

"Only these seeds," I said, "& all exceedingly small."
My friend scratched where the trap had bitten him years ago,
& a steady stream of green ants carried a moth wing

across the footpath. It passed like a sail or a fin.
"Break one," he said. "Now what do you see?"
I split open a seed with the edge of my thumbnail,

cupped it in the palms of my hands & squinted
under the smoky light slanting downward
through the treetops. There was a very small tree

folded up inside, with one pale leaf on a stem
the length of an eyelash. It sprang to life
& put out hundreds of jackfruit blossoms all at once

but when I started to speak they blew everywhere.

NINTH CIRCLE

What demon possessed me that I behaved so well?

THOREAU

I. THE INTERPRETER

Two rifles led the way through mustard grass.
It sprang back where they passed with the hush
of skirts swept over a threshold. A threshold of glass,

a chapel of sand giving onto a landscape of ash.
We passed through. Slow down, said the boy
on the stretcher. We'd stopped for a smoke in the brush

& he lay with his head on a stone, staring up at the sky.
A beetle crawled over his chest. Slow down please,
he said. It flicked open its wings like a wind-up toy

but didn't fly off like a toy. On my knees,
things seemed less tragic. It was raining as always.
The mustard grass screened a light breeze

from the east. I had nothing clever to say,
so I lit up & told him the tale of my ivory pipe.
Near the end of the story, its maker betrays

the pipe's secret location (inside a tin cup at the top
of his pack) by his refusal to serve our men tea.
Manners, I said, will save a man's life. The quiet type,

he kept his eyes on the sky. He said Please.

II. LUCK

Next we came to yoked bullocks champing on thistles
though our charts showed no settlement in that sector.
As per my instructions I blew hard on the whistle,

calling to shore. A figure emerged. We cut the motor.
She waded in up to her knees through the shallows
lifting her hem so the depth wouldn't wreck her

dirty blue smock. The crew cheered her on, though
by now you could see she was pock-marked & simple
& we already had a nice girl in the hold. Our prow

caught in hyacinths. She lifted that smock stippled
with rust-colored roses while old men on deck
took turns flipping coins at a three-legged table.

The youngest kept winning. I'd called it luck,
the luck of old men in a boat, but they called it fate.
It was tails. Tails again. The losers kept scratching their necks

& rubbing their beards when they lost, which of late
was all day. I pointed her out to these men. The oldest
was scarred by the plague & would know it on sight.

He flipped the coin. Tails again. I started the motor.

III. CANISTERS

We took samples. The captain's boy groaned at the winch
as another black canister rose from the river & swung
up our hull with each crank. He had a nice touch,

all agreed. It was darker now—heavy with river, hung
in mid-air from a coppery cord. Men heaved it on board
to cap it, freeze it, label, rack & stack it among

the 'priority' samples, then bolted the heavy steel doors
to the frozen compartment. I'd always liked it in there.
Sealed off from jungle, blue tiles on the sterilized floor

reflecting one's self underfoot in the halogen glare.
A good place to think. I cracked open yesterday's canister.
Out slid a cartridge of ice; it fell in my lap. Taking care

not to melt it I lifted it up though my fingers blistered
with cold. The overhead bulb shone clear through,
gilding each bubble of air locked inside with a lustre

not its own. So this is the river. It looks almost blue.
Blue-green, depending on lighting. Let's call it green,
green-blue with flecks. Under a leaf, something grows

near the defrosting surface, its eyelids so thin
you can see to the pupils beneath. You can see
the veins networking under the skin,

each filament threading its way to the dark-chambered seed
in the ribs. It's losing its tail. It's growing a face.
Pity the river-god learning to breathe.

IV. HOME

Night fell on my watch. Into the night, night fell.
She fell hard & took my face in her broken hands;
she told me I was facing home. It was hard to tell,

as a child can't tell if he's turned to the nightstand
or the fleur-de-lis papered wall in his waking
but still-closed eyes. He wakes to the sound

of somebody beating a rug on the terrace. Thinking,
My heart, you have brought me this far.
I don't even know if it's over or not. If I'm waiting

or not. I don't even know how to wait in the dark.

V. THE PLANET

A flunky mops auroras
of spilled oil from the deck.
Green scrim, gray corolla,

badge of rust. Once I examined a speck
that color in the night. An old man held
his spyglass to my eye until I picked

it out, gray whiskers at my ear, hands the smell
of soil. We were adrift. He pointed out
three moons & a storm that was older

than Man on its face. He's dead, no doubt,
old man. A blast inside a fleck, a storm
you can't imagine though you see it blow about

so calmly in the lens. The river swarms
with dragonflies. It hurts
to look in this light, at ripples like torn

foil & change changing the dirt
to milky earth at river's edge. It's the sun,
it's affecting my eyes. At first,

I thought it was something I'd done.

SCARECROW ECLOGUE

Then I took the poem in my hand & walked out
past the well & three levelled acres
to where the sugarcane built itself slowly to the songs of
    immature goats
& there at the field's shimmering center

I inserted the page
into the delicately-woven grass of the scarecrow's upraised hand
where it began to shine & give a little in the gentle
unremitting breeze sent over from the east.

I stepped back several paces
to look at what I'd done.
Only a little way off & the morning light bleached out my ink
on the page so it simplified

into a white rectangle against a skyblue field
flapping once, twice
as if grazed by one close shot after another.
The oxen snorted nearby

& there was a sense of publication
but not much else was different, so I backed off all the way
to the sugarcane's edge until the poem was only a gleam
among the fieldworkers' sickles surfacing

like the silver backs of dolphins
up above the green crop-rows into view, then down from view.
How it shone in my withdrawal,
worksongs rising

over it all. So then I said the poem aloud, my version
of what the god dressed up as a charioteer said
to the reluctant bowman
at the center of the battlefield.

How he spoke of duty, the substance
of this world,
& the trembling armies ranged.

FIFTH CIRCLE

Tap tap, you've posted a scarecrow
at the center of your field
of broken stones. Watch it grow,

watch it blow. You've nailed
her to the desolation tree
blossoming over this field

where somebody buried a seed
long ago. Bone hammer,
crooked hammer, thing nailed to a tree.

This is what love would look like.
This is what home would look like,
if only you'd look. You look

away. The sunset a smear
on a stone, a smutted gown,
silhouettes ploughing the dark near

the hem. You rag doll. You clown,
you tatter at twilight. Soiled
little prince, what have you done?

What have you done to our field?

WAITING FOR THE ECLIPSE
IN THE BLACK GARDEN

It takes long.

A wind comes worrying the candle-tip.

Our servant's teeth flicker.

His jawbone flickers.

Once I watched him cut open a goat.

Now no one can breathe.

The black disc locks into place.

Listen. Listen.

Under that box is a snake.

Listen while the unlit places hollow you out.

MONSOON ECLOGUE

Some years ago a procession
of men calling themselves
the sky-clad came
to this district to build
a hospital for birds that had been
damaged by the rains.

The landholders here
my grandfather among them
decided against it —
it not being our way
to intervene with monsoons

which is why to this day
the birds here grow
so damaged & wise,

or so our tutor said gravely

before stepping out into the sun-
washed coriander patch to watch
droplets work down
stems one by one, small
storms suspended, while over
the rooftiles came
breakers of mist making
our whole house to him
drift back like the high prow

of the viceroy's steamship
he watched sail off with his youth.

Inside I still could not find
the main verb the chariot
wheel performed. I thought

it was silver. It bore

the king with 100 heads
across a battlefield red
with his wounded
up to the end of the
beginner's workbook

then blue-skinned Rama bent his bow then his
raider's arrow met
the axle & then

I could not stop laughing

as through the doorway my mother scolded
the aphasic houseboy

who peed into our
green watertank
(black putti, untouchable)
arcing the thin golden
stream & singing
ooo-ee ooo-ee at our ruin.

The grammatical rules of this language can be learned in one sitting.

Nouns have no gender & end in -o; the plural terminates in -oj (pronounced -oy) & the accusative, -on (plural -ojn).

Amiko, friend; amikoj, friends; amikon & amikojn, accusative friend & friends.

Adjectives end in —a & take plural & accusative endings to agree with things.

Ma amiko is my friend.

All verbs are regular & have only one form for each tense or mood; they are not altered for person or number. Mi havas bonajn amikojn is simply to say I have good friends.

Adverbs end in —e.

La bonaj amiko estas ie. The good friend is here.

▬

A new book appears in Esperanto every week. Radio stations in Europe, the United States, China, Russia & Brazil broadcast in Esperanto, as does Vatican Radio. In 1959, UNESCO declared the International Federation of Esperanto Speakers to be in accord with its mission & granted this body consultative status. The youth branch of the International Federation of Esperanto Speakers, UTA, has offices in 80 different countries & organizes social events where young people curious about the movement may dance to recordings by Esperanto artists, enjoy complimentary soft drinks & take home Esperanto versions of major literary works including the Old Testament & *A Midsummer Night's Dream*. William Shatner's first feature-length vehicle was a horror film shot entirely in Esperanto. Esperanto is among the languages currently sailing into deep space on board the Voyager spacecraft.

—

Esperanto is an artificial language
constructed in 1887 by L.
   L. Zamenhof, a Polish
      oculist. I first came
across *Fundamento Esperanto,* the text
   which introduced this system
       to the world, as I travelled abroad

following a somewhat difficult period
in my life. It was twilight & snowing on the
   railway platform just outside
     Warsaw where I had missed
my connection. A man in a crumpled track suit
   & dark glasses pushed a cart
       piled high with ripped & weathered volumes —

sex manuals, detective stories, yellowing
musical scores & outdated physics textbooks,
   old copies of *Life,* new smut,
     an atlas translated,

a grammar, *The Mirror,* Soviet-bloc comics,
   a guide to the rivers &
        mountains, thesauri, inscrutable

musical scores & mimeographed physics books,
defective stories, obsolete sex manuals —
     one of which caught my notice
     (Dr. Esperanto,
Zamenhof's pen name, translates as He Who Hopes) &
   since I had time, I traded
     my used *Leaves of Grass* for a copy.

Mi amas vin, bela amiko.
I'm afraid I will never be lonely enough.
There's a man from Quebec in my head,

a friend to the purple martins.
Purple martins are the Cadillac of swallows.
All purple martins are dying or dead.
Brainscans of grown purple martins suggest
these creatures feel the same levels of doubt

& bliss as an eight-year-old girl in captivity.
While driving home from the brewery
one night this man from Quebec heard a radio program
about purple martins & the next day he set out
to build them a house

in his own back yard. I've never built anything,
let alone a house,

not to mention a home
for somebody else.

I've never unrolled a blueprint onto a workbench,
sunk a post,
or sent the neighbor's kid pedalling off
to the store for a bag full of nails.

I've never waited ten years for a swallow.

Never put in aluminum floors to smooth over the waiting.
Never piped sugar water through colored tubes
to each empty nest lined with newspaper shredded
with strong, tired hands.
Never dismantled the entire affair

& put it back together again.
Still no swallows.
I never installed the big light that stays on through the night

to keep owls away. Never installed lesser lights,
never rested on Sunday

with a beer on the deck surveying
what I had done
& what yet remained to be done, listening to Styx

while the neighbor kids ran through my sprinklers.
I have never collapsed in abandon.
Never prayed.
But enough about purple martins.

░

As we speak, Esperanto is being corrupted
by upstart languages such as Interlingua,
Klingon, Java & various cryptophasic tongues.

Our only hope of reversing this trend is to write
the Esperanto epic. Through its grandeur
& homegrown humility, it will spur men

to freeze the mutating patois so the children
of our children's children may dwell in this song
& find comfort in its true texture & frame.

It's worth a try. As I imagine it, it ends
in the middle of things. Every line of the work
is a first & a last line & this is the spring

of its action. Of course, there's a journey
& inside that journey, an implicit voyage
through the underworld. There's a bridge

made of boats; a carp stuffed with flowers;
a comic dispute among sweetmeat vendors;
a digression on shadows; men clapping

in fields to scare away crows; an unending list
of warships: *The Unternehmen, The Impresa,*
The Muyarchi, Viec Lam, The Przedsiebiorstwo,

The Indarka, The Enterprise, L'Entreprise,
Entrepreno. . . One could go on. But by now,
all the characters have turned into swallows

& bank as one flock in the sky—that is,
all except one. That's how we finally learn
who the hero was all along. Weary & old,

he sits on a rock & watches his friends
fly one by one out of the song,
then turns back to the journey they all began

long ago, keeping the river to his right.

FOURTH CIRCLE

Fig tree stamped
on the back of a
coin. Sticky fig I
swapped for a coin
in my prime. O
coin I bought with
a coin in my age.

Fame & famine must spring from one root. From salt comes our soldier. While one tribe makes merry, another invents the wheeled chariot & alas nothing can stop it. Modern man walks in the garden of its turbulence. Modern man walks in the shadow of the rider, the raider whose doom is this dim marble mood. The gallery closes at eight. The station at twelve. Then the taps, then the first cabaret. I've sewn the ribbons back onto your bodice, now rip it off again, only slowly this time & with feeling. We've got five minutes to go. Outside the Hotel Cassiopeia, the moon scribbles white on a dark, moving surface. The mulberry branch on my dresser ramifies through the night. At this hour, it's hard to tell blossoms from silkworms inventing their shrouds. Verily. Yea, verily.

THIRD CIRCLE

Along with the bitter, burnt onions,
the glazed livers of cattle, chattel
of what's past, we ruminated the dawn

on that slope, blown wort rattling
its seed under barrelsome bellies
big with the promise of capital

for Fall. Dapple drops to her knees
for the very first time & lows,
blinks & thinks moo, it's blurry,

the open, with its one-armed tree
waving welcome to the sensorium,
trunk sunk like a bolt in jade meadow.

Hello hello, make yourself a home.
Our Apple licks young Dapple clean
under placental skies, a cerise dome,

dulcet Dapple. Funny, this sweet
without sweetness. Come from within,
next thing you know she's up on her feet

with her lips to some visitor's hand.

ON DIFFICULTY

Suffer yourself to know beautiful women.
Suffer yourself to learn many words
for one thing. Suffer yourself

to elope like a river, suffer yourself
to remain. Are there ways to kill time
without hurting eternity?

Me, I make seagulls from paper.
Once you've mastered the folds (valley crease,
rabbit's ear), everything

tucks itself in. How crooked rooftops
enfold sleeping souls under stars
seems so simple. Pagodas

in traffic lights, birds within birds
without end. When she left, she left me
this note on the table.

I can't make anything of it.

WELKIN

Stretch out a blank. Prime it, fashion it robin's-egg blue. Step back & regard the impression: square cut out of the sea, tile plucked from the floor of a waiting room. Add custard & copper. Next come the pioneer slashes of onset, working up from the bottom as in life. Think flamingo in the abattoir. Think glory. Build lilacs & lavish the madder. Then throw the thing out & start over. This indigo here comes from India. This peacock from spinach. Now start your dark at the edges, working inward with artful gradations. Be sure to go back & strew it all over with spangles. Take down the easel & hold up your night.

SEVENTH CIRCLE

It may be useful to think of a patterned carpet made up of repeating units of the same design. If one meditates upon any individual spiral, the silence churns with texture & shape. Viewed on a large scale, however, one swathe looks exactly like another. In this sense, the universe has no structure at all. Toward the end of the century, mankind carried out a detailed audit of the Coma Cluster. They found that one quarter of its weight was made up of baryons. This came as a terrible surprise. You see, our cosmos is largely composed of invisible particles. Therefore it follows. To render yourself transparent, it is needful to fashion a small image in the form of a man. The beginner is cautioned against using blood unless prayers & pentacles fail. On a starless night, write the following characters with a needle upon the skull. What remains is unseen.

GRYPHON

Count that man fortunate who happens across but one gryphon in his lifetime. Fortunate, insofar as this creature is said to assemble her unearthly eyrie of beryl & jasper in the most august bestiaries. As a boy, I used to pass twilights surveying the ether for gryphons beyond our back yard. Father frowned skyward & sipped from his tumbler as he told me their ways. They shit gold. They carry off sailors. When one weeps by the defrauded nest it's like watching a high rise collapse, but I never saw it. Now that I'm old, I wish my heart had lit on more probable game from the start. To wit, the sylph. Mark my words, gryphons are shy & troublesome creatures, hardly worth hitching your handcart of hopes to. Moreover, they tear men to pieces.

ACID HOUSE

after George Issakidis

You may stretch a note culled from the call of the ruby-throated warbler into some banshee's unspeakable song. Likewise, extended events like this recording of the Qur'an can be digitally compressed until surrender sounds like one beat of a kick drum. Every beat is the kingdom. Every beat is a helix of clusters of verses on various matters — how to kneel, how to keep bees in the desert — each verse implying the unearthly system even if it can be sung in one breath. It has no beginning or end. It is infinite, or rather, a window onto the infinite. It is daybreak. The window is cracked & so is the sunrise beyond. In here it's all darkness & everything rattles to monoliths booming on tripods. We sway though no harlequin raves in the slab.

SONNET

I was cold.
You wove me a mantle of smoke.
I was thirsty.
You sent me a cloud in a crate.
You sent me a note.
You sent me a crate in a crate with a note saying bury this.
So I struck off with my shovel & never came back.
When the digging was over, I buried my shovel.
I buried it deeper.
Tendered my prospects to dusk.
Some men will make a grave out of anything.
Anything.
It depends on how lonely they get.
Times when a body could dig through the night.

PALINODE

There is no Ursula, Ursula. Never was there any balcony braving the waves. Nothing was promised, no buttons undone. There's only this silence lit by a dangling bulb & some woman's cracked voice hissing Silence. I regret to inform you that there is no reason for tears. No horses were slain at Magenta. Birkenau was not named for birches. No serfs reached the sea, no cuttlefish died for this light. If you were to crawl to me across this great marble chamber with its hallways & crooked columns of volumes, I might reconsider. That would be reason for tears, but no Ursula crawls. No paramour whores herself under these trestles. When it gets lonely, I sit by the river & read. Correction. There is no river. Mostly, I read.

ARIA

The ending is sad if you think of it.
Portable castle, luna,

two singers pretending to kiss
for the mob. Ovation. The end

of applause, the sound of a fire
beginning to flag in the dark.

Somebody took down the bay
& left us to pick up the boats

in the pit. Rigging everywhere.
What stagecraft, what dripping

cathedrals. I sit on my rock
with a fistful of raisins

& listen. Sometimes an extra
dismantles a cloud. Sometimes

a whale remembers the spotlight.

CORRUPTION (II)

In one of Grimm's stories, a little tailor defeats a giant in a throwing contest by lofting a bird in the air. Happily ever after arrives, but the bird never lands. She flies straight out of the tale. Tonight, a vessel catapults through the heavens with a gold-plated phonograph fixed to its side. In less than forty thousand years this craft will drift through the nearest system, bearing greetings in fifty-seven languages, including the encoded song of the humpback whale. By then our tongue will have crossed into extinction or changed utterly. Lately, I have taken an interest in words like "here." Here was a chapel, for instance. Here is a footprint filling with rain. Here might be enough. Could not the same be said of elsewhere? Yes, I suppose. But I know precious little of elsewhere.

NOTES

The "Corruption" poems occasionally adapt, or 'corrupt,' language and ideas from Saint Augustine's *Confessions*, W. G. Sebald's *The Rings of Saturn*, and Simone Weil's essay "Forms of the Implicit Love of God."

The "Circle" poems obliquely revisit the ethical landscape of Dante's *Inferno*.

Information on the grammar and social history of Esperanto in the poem "Fundamentals of Esperanto" was drawn from various websites on the internet.

The lines "Are there ways to kill time/without hurting eternity?" from "On Difficulty" slightly reword an aphorism of Thoreau's in *Walden*.

"Fundamentals of Esperanto" is for Pierre Guertin.

ACKNOWLEDGMENTS

Grateful acknowledgment is made to the editors of the journals in which the following poems first appeared, often in different versions:

"Fundamentals of Esperanto": *American Poetry Review* 32: 4 (July/August 2003).

"First Circle," "Second Circle": *Fence* 5: 1 (2002).

"Evening with Stars" (originally titled "Corruption"): *Grand Street* 18: 2 (2002).

"Monsoon Eclogue": *The Harvard Review* 22 (2002).

"Jungle Book," "Sixth Circle" (originally titled "Reel"): *Lit* 3: 2 (2002).

"Centaur": *Octopus* 2 (Fall 2003).

"Fifth Circle," "Eighth Circle": *Ploughshares* 27: 4 (Winter 2001–2002).

"Acid House," "Seventh Circle" (originally titled "Grimoire"), "Welkin," "Raven & Eclipse": *Slope* 15 (Summer 2002).

"Inner Life": *Upstairs at Duroc* 5: 6 (2001–2002).

"Aria," "Third Circle," "Corruption," "Hotel Lullaby," "Loose Strife with Apiary," "Sonnet": *Verse* 20:1 (2003).

"Burial Practice": *Volt* 9 (2003).

"Corruption" also appeared in the anthology *Short Fuse: A Global Anthology* (Rattapallax Press, 2002).

"Monsoon Eclogue" was also featured on the *Poetry Daily* website (July 30, 2002).

"Aria," "Hotel Lullaby," "Sonnet," and "Third Circle" were also featured in *Jacket* 19.

Thanks to my family, friends, and teachers for their love and guidance during the writing of this book.